A Journey of Understanding and Empowerment

Unmasking

Autism

Embracing the Solution to Unlock the Potential Within.

Authored By: Dr Devon Hunt

Copyright © 2023 by Dr. Devon Hunt

All Rights Reserved.

No part of this book may be used or reproduced by any means, graphic, electronic, or mechanical, including photocopying, recording, taping, or by any information storage retrieval system without the written permission of the publisher.

Contents.

Introduction
What is Autism?

Chapter 1:
The Masked Reality

Chapter 2
Breaking Through Barriers

Chapter 3
The Power of Understanding

Chapter 4
Embracing Neurodiversity

Chapter 5:
Unlocking the Solution

Chapter 6
A Future of Empowerment

Conclusion

Introduction

Life Experience Story:

Unmasking Autism: A Journey of Understanding and Empowerment is a deeply personal account that chronicles my experience as a Father, Doctor, caregiver, and advocate for individuals on the autism spectrum. Through this book, I aim to shed light on the challenges faced by those affected by autism and provide insights into the solutions that can transform lives.

As a parent, when my child was first diagnosed with autism, I found myself thrust into a world of uncertainty and confusion. I grappled with the overwhelming emotions, unanswered questions, and societal stigmas surrounding the condition. It was during this journey that I discovered the power of understanding, acceptance, and embracing neurodiversity.

Throughout the pages of Unmasking Autism, I invite readers to join me on an introspective journey where we peel back the layers of misunderstanding and misconception surrounding autism. Together, we will navigate the intricate landscape of diagnosis, education, and social integration, all while uncovering the hidden strengths, talents, and potential that lie within individuals on the spectrum.

Drawing from scientific research, personal anecdotes, and the experiences of other families, this book aims to bridge the gap between the autism community and the world at large. It seeks to foster empathy, awareness, and compassion, while advocating for a society that embraces and empowers every individual, regardless of their neurodivergence.

Unmasking Autism goes beyond simply raising awareness; it offers tangible solutions and strategies for supporting individuals with autism in various aspects of their lives. From education and employment to communication and social interactions, this book delves into the practical steps that can be taken to create inclusive environments and promote the overall well-being of those on the autism spectrum.

Ultimately, Unmasking Autism is a call to action. It serves as a rallying cry for parents, caregivers, educators, and policymakers to work together, break down barriers, and build a world where individuals with autism can thrive and fulfill their potential. It is my hope that by sharing my story and the stories of others, we can inspire a collective transformation that will lead to a more inclusive and understanding society.

So, join me on this journey of discovery, as we unmask the true essence of autism and uncover the boundless possibilities that lie within. Together, let us embrace the solution and create a world where every individual on the spectrum can live a life of dignity, empowerment, and fulfillment.

What is Autism?

Autism, also known as Autism Spectrum Disorder (ASD), is a neurodevelopmental disorder that affects how a person perceives and interacts with the world around them. It is characterized by a range of challenges in social skills, communication, and repetitive behaviors. Autism is considered a spectrum disorder because it varies widely in its presentation and severity, with each individual experiencing a unique combination of symptoms and strengths.

The exact cause of autism is still not fully understood, but it is believed to involve a combination of genetic and environmental factors. It is not caused by parenting practices or vaccines, as once mistakenly believed.

The core features of autism typically manifest in early childhood, although diagnosis may occur later in some cases. These features can include:

1. Social and communication difficulties: Individuals with autism often have difficulty understanding and responding to social cues, such as facial expressions, tone of voice, and body language. They may struggle with developing and maintaining relationships, and have challenges in initiating and sustaining conversations.

2. Restricted and repetitive behaviors: People with autism may engage in repetitive movements or behaviors, such as hand-flapping, rocking, or specific rituals and routines. They may also have intense interests in certain topics and exhibit a strong desire for sameness and predictability in their environment.

3. Sensory sensitivities: Many individuals with autism have heightened sensitivity or hypo-sensitivity to sensory input, such as loud noises, bright lights, or certain textures. This can lead to sensory overload or withdrawal in certain situations.

It is important to note that individuals with autism also have unique strengths and abilities. Some may excel in areas such as attention to detail, visual thinking, and problem-solving. With the right support and accommodations, individuals with autism can make significant progress in their development and lead fulfilling lives.

Early intervention, such as behavioral therapy, speech therapy, and occupational therapy, can be beneficial in addressing the challenges associated with autism. Individualized education plans, sensory supports, and social skills training are often implemented to provide appropriate support in academic and social settings.

It is crucial for society to foster acceptance, inclusion, and understanding of individuals with autism. By promoting awareness and creating supportive environments, we can help individuals on the autism spectrum thrive and reach their full potential.

Chapter 1:

The Masked Reality

Let's delve into the initial stages of discovering and understanding autism. Mask Reality focuses on the hidden aspects of autism that may not be immediately evident, and the journey of unraveling its presence and impact.

In this chapter, we explore several key elements:

1. The First Signs:

The first signs of autism vary from person to person, but they often appear in early childhood. Recognizing these signs is important for early intervention and support. Common early signs of autism are:

1. Difficulties in social communication:

Children with autism can have difficulty interacting socially. They may have limited eye contact, difficulty understanding and responding to social cues, difficulty initiating and maintaining conversations, and lack of interest in peer interaction.

2. Delayed or atypical language development:
Language delay and atypical language development are common early signs of autism. Some children are slow to speak, while others have developed language skills but have difficulty communicating using language. They may repeat words and phrases (echolaria) and have a limited vocabulary.

3. Repetitive Behaviors and Limited Interests:
Children with autism often exhibit repetitive behaviors such as: B. Shaking hands, shaking hands, rotating objects, or repeating certain actions or actions. They may also show a strong interest in certain topics, objects, or activities and exclude others.

4. Senses:

Many people with autism have sensory hypersensitivity or sensory processing differences. Hypersensitivity or hypersensitivity to certain sensory stimuli such as sound, light, texture, taste, or smell may occur. They may show disgust or seek sensory input in certain ways.

5. Lack of roleplay or imagination:
Children with autism may have difficulty participating in role-plays and imaginative activities. They may have difficulty understanding or participating in imaginative or symbolic play scenarios, preferring more concrete, literal interactions.

It is important to note that these signs may vary in severity and appearance. Some children may have more pronounced symptoms, while others may have milder or more subtle symptoms. If parents or caregivers notice concerns about their child's development, they are encouraged to consult with a health care professional or specialist experienced in diagnosing and treating autism spectrum disorders. Early detection and intervention can make a big difference in helping people with autism reach their full potential.

2. Seeking Answers:

When parents and caregivers notice signs and behaviors that may indicate autism in their child, they often seek answers and gain a better understanding of their child's condition. This process of finding answers involves various steps and actions.

1. Identify your concerns.
The first step is to acknowledge that your child's development and behavior may be different or worrying. Parents and caregivers may notice behavioral patterns and developmental milestones not being met and seek additional information and guidance.

2. Research and information gathering:
Parents often begin researching and gathering information about autism as soon as concerns arise. You can read books, articles, her resources online, and get advice from

trusted sources such as medical professionals and her support groups. This information-seeking stage helps you gain a basic understanding of autism and its characteristics.

3. Medical consultation:

Parents can schedule an appointment with a medical professional, such as a pediatrician or developmental specialist, to discuss their concerns and obtain an expert opinion. These professionals can assess, screen, and evaluate your child to determine if they meet diagnostic criteria for autism.

4. Diagnostic process:

The diagnostic process typically includes a comprehensive evaluation by a multidisciplinary team that includes psychologists, speech therapists, occupational therapists, and other specialists. We may administer a variety of tests and assessments to assess your child's behavior, communication skills, social interactions and developmental milestones. This process aims to provide a formal diagnosis and a deeper understanding of your child's strengths and challenges.

5. Seek professional help.

Once diagnosed, parents can seek ongoing professional support and intervention. This may include working with therapists, counselors and professional educators who can provide strategies and therapies tailored to your child's specific needs.

6. Connectivity to support networks:

Parents can also seek connections with support networks such as autism advocacy groups, parent support groups, and online communities. These networks provide a sense of community, understanding and guidance in overcoming the challenges of raising a child with autism.

Finding answers is a positive and important step in understanding and helping children with autism. It gives parents and guardians access to resources, professional advice and support networks that can contribute to the well-being and development of their children. Seeking answers gives families a clearer picture of their child's unique strengths and challenges, leading to effective interventions and support strategies.

3. Unveiling Emotions:

Families may experience a range of emotions when a child is diagnosed with autism. Uncovering these feelings and working through them is an important part of the journey. Here are some common feelings individuals and families experience after receiving an autism diagnosis.

1. Confusion:

Confusion may be your first reaction to being diagnosed with autism. Parents may have questions about what autism means for their child's future, what causes it, and how it affects family relationships. Understanding the complexity of autism and its implications can be overwhelming and confusing.

2. Refusal:

Denial is a common emotional reaction when faced with a difficult diagnosis. Parents may find it difficult to accept that their child has autism, hoping it is just a stage or misunderstanding. It can take time to process and accept the reality of your diagnosis.

3. Fear:

A diagnosis of autism is often accompanied by anxiety. Parents may worry about their child's future, their ability to reach developmental milestones, and the challenges they may face in society. Anxiety may arise from concerns about obtaining appropriate education, treatment, and support services.

4. sorrow:

Knowing that your child has autism can be sad and heartbreaking. Parents may lament the loss of the expectations they had for their child's development and the experiences of a "normal" childhood. It is important to recognize and process these feelings of grief.

5. Grief:

Being diagnosed with autism can cause parents to grieve for the loss of the future they envisioned for their child, triggering a grieving process. It's important to give space to this grief and seek support to manage the emotions that come with it.

6. Acceptance:

Over time, individuals and families may reach a stage of acceptance. Acceptance does not mean giving up on children or their potential, it means embracing and understanding autism as a unique part of life. It's about leveraging the child's strengths, meeting their needs, and focusing on their growth and development.

7. Hope:

Along with other emotions, there is often an emotion of hope. Families are beginning to realize that a child's diagnosis opens the door to early interventions, support networks and resources that can positively impact the child's development. Hope is the driving force behind finding the right interventions to work on your child's progress.

Dealing with these feelings requires time, support and understanding. It is important for individuals and families to seek emotional support, such as counseling and therapy, to help them process their emotions and develop coping strategies. Sharing experiences with other families who have had similar experiences can also provide reassurance, support and guidance.

Ultimately, the journey towards coming to terms with and accepting the reality of autism leads to a sense of self-determination and a focus on the unique strengths and abilities of people with autism.

4. The Impact on Family:

When someone in the family is diagnosed with autism, it has a huge impact on the whole family. The challenges and adaptations associated with autism can affect family relationships, relationships, and daily life. Here are some key aspects of how autism affects families.

1. Emotional impact:

A diagnosis of autism can evoke a range of emotions in families. Parents may feel shocked, sad, guilty, and worried about their child's future. Siblings can have mixed emotions, including confusion, frustration, and concern for their siblings. It's important for families to find healthy ways to support each other and deal with these feelings.

2. Changed priority:

The needs of a child with autism often require adjustments in family priorities. Families may need to devote more time, energy, and resources to treatment, interventions, and educational support. This shift in priorities can affect work-life balance, financial planning, and social activities within the family.

3. Changes in family relationships:

Autism can affect family relationships. Parents can face increased stress and pressure when dealing with the challenges of raising a child with special needs. Siblings may have to adjust to their role as siblings of children with autism, which can bring both rewards and challenges. It is important for families to create an inclusive and supportive environment that considers the needs of all family members.

4. Financial Considerations:
Autism-related costs, such as therapy sessions, professional training, and medical procedures, can put a strain on household budgets. Families may need to arrange insurance, seek financial assistance, or adjust budgets to meet the needs of their child with autism.

5. Relationship Impact:
Relationships between partners and family members can be strained due to the need to care for a child with autism. Stress, fatigue, and emotional problems can increase tension and make communication difficult. It's important that families maintain open communication, seek support, and prioritize self-care to strengthen relationships.

6. Strengthen advocacy:

Families of children with autism are often strong advocates for their children's needs. We may need to work with the education system, health care system and community resources to ensure that your child receives appropriate support and services. Advocacy can be time consuming and difficult, but it can also enable families to make a positive impact in a child's life.

Although challenging, the impact of autism on families can also foster resilience, compassion, and personal growth. Families learn to appreciate small victories, celebrate their unique strengths, and find joy in shared experiences. Building a support network, accessing respite care, and finding community resources can provide valuable support and reduce the burden on families. In summary, the impact of autism on families is significant and varied. It influences emotions, priorities, power relations, financial situations, relationships, and advocacy needs. By recognizing and managing these effects, families can work together to overcome the challenges of autism and create a supportive and nurturing environment for the whole family.

5. Confronting Stigma:

Explore the social stigma surrounding autism and the challenges individuals and families face in facing and overcoming autism. Stigma refers to negative attitudes, stereotypes, and discrimination that may be associated with autism.

1. Misconceptions and stereotypes:
Discuss misconceptions and stereotypes surrounding autism. These may include believing that people with autism are less intelligent, lack empathy, or are incapable of living a fulfilling life. We emphasize the importance of dispelling these misconceptions and disseminating accurate information about autism.

2. Social exclusion and isolation:
People with autism and their families often experience social exclusion and isolation because of the stigma associated with autism. We address challenges they face in social settings, such as difficulties making friends,

participating in community activities, and accessing comprehensive educational and recreational opportunities.

3. Ignorance and Ignorance:
We address the lack of understanding and awareness of autism that perpetuates stigma. This section highlights the need for education and awareness campaigns to promote more inclusive and tolerant societies.

4. Statements of interest and self-representations:
We emphasize the importance of advocacy for people with autism and their families. We discuss the efforts of advocates to challenge stigmatizing attitudes and promote acceptance, inclusion and equal opportunity. It also explores the concept of self-advocacy, which gives people with autism the opportunity to express their needs, rights and desires.

5. Promote acceptance and inclusion:
We emphasize the importance of promoting acceptance and inclusion of people with autism. This includes creating inclusive environments in schools, workplaces and

communities where people with autism are valued for their unique strengths and contributions. We will discuss efforts to promote neurodiversity and encourage societal acceptance of the differences and abilities of people with autism.

6. Change your perception:
We explore the possibility of changing perceptions of autism and reducing stigma. We emphasize the importance of personal stories, media exposure and public awareness campaigns in changing social attitudes and fostering acceptance.

By combating stigma, individuals and families affected by autism can work towards building a more inclusive and understanding society. This section encourages readers to challenge stereotypes, educate others, advocate for change, and promote acceptance and inclusion of people with autism.

6. Embracing the Journey:

This section explores the process of embracing your journey with autism, with a focus on finding moments of clarity, acceptance, and empowerment. This highlights the strength and resilience individuals and families have as they overcome the challenges of autism. Here's a breakdown of the key points covered in this section:

1. Seek understanding:

Discuss the importance of seeking understanding for autism. This includes learning about the symptoms, their characteristics, and available resources. Through learning, individuals and families can gain a deeper understanding of their experiences and develop effective support strategies.

2. Praise your strengths:

We emphasize the importance of recognizing and celebrating the unique strengths and abilities of people with autism. This section highlights the many talents that autistic people can have, such as exceptional memory, attention to detail, creativity, and analytical thinking.

Focusing on strengths helps individuals build confidence and tap into their abilities.

3. Building a support network:

Discuss the value of building a support network, such as connecting with other family members, joining an autism support group, or seeking professional help. These networks allow individuals and families to share experiences and learn from each other by providing emotional support, guidance and a sense of belonging.

4. Encourage self-care:

We emphasize the importance of self-care for individuals and families affected by autism. Taking care of your physical, emotional and mental health is important to staying resilient and meeting the challenges of travel. We explore strategies for self-care. These include practicing mindfulness, seeking tranquility, and participating in activities that bring joy and relaxation.

5. Set realistic expectations.

Discuss the importance of setting realistic expectations for people with autism. This includes understanding that progress can happen at different rates and in different areas for different people. By leveraging individual strengths and focusing on personal growth, individuals and families can create a positive and supportive environment.

6. Advocacy and Entitlement:

We emphasize the power of advocacy and assertiveness in working with autism. This includes advocating for appropriate education and community support and enabling people with autism to express their needs, preferences and aspirations. By becoming an advocate, individuals and families can make a positive impact on themselves and the lives of others. 7. Find joy and gratitude:

We explore the importance of finding joy and gratitude in our journey with autism. This section focuses on celebrating small victories, cherishing moments of connection and progress, and expressing gratitude for the love and support you receive. Encourages individuals and families to find happiness and fulfillment in the midst of hardship.

By embarking on a journey with autism, individuals and families can build resilience, find strength in unique experiences, and build meaningful and fulfilling lives. This section encourages readers to approach this journey with an open mind, a positive attitude, and a commitment to self-care and advocacy.

Chapter 2

Breaking Through Barriers

Breaking through barriers is a critical aspect of navigating the challenges of autism and achieving personal growth and success. In this section, we explore the concept of breaking through barriers and provide an explanation of its significance.

Here's an overview:

1. Barriers:
Barriers refer to obstacles or challenges that individuals with autism encounter in their daily lives. These barriers can impede their progress, limit opportunities, and hinder their ability to fully participate in society. Here's a concise explanation of some common barriers faced by individuals with autism:

1. Communication Barriers: Many individuals with autism experience difficulties in communication. They may have

challenges in expressing themselves verbally, understanding social cues, or using nonverbal communication effectively. These communication barriers can affect their ability to express their needs, interact with others, and form meaningful connections.

2. Social Barriers: Social interactions can be challenging for individuals with autism due to difficulties in understanding social norms, reading facial expressions, or interpreting social cues. They may struggle with making friends, engaging in conversations, or understanding the unspoken rules of social interactions. These social barriers can lead to feelings of isolation and exclusion.

3. Sensory Barriers: Individuals with autism often have sensory sensitivities, which can be barriers to their participation in various environments. They may be hypersensitive or hyposensitive to certain sensory stimuli such as noise, touch, or lights. These sensitivities can cause discomfort, distress, or sensory overload, making it challenging for them to navigate different settings.

4. Educational Barriers: Accessing appropriate education can be a barrier for individuals with autism. They may require specialized instruction, individualized supports, and accommodations to meet their unique learning needs. However, limited resources, lack of inclusive practices, and inadequate support systems can pose barriers to accessing quality education.

5. Employment Barriers: Finding and maintaining employment can be challenging for individuals with autism due to various factors. Employers may have limited understanding of autism, leading to misconceptions and biases during the hiring process. Additionally, difficulties with social skills, sensory sensitivities, and inflexible work environments can present barriers to successful employment.

6. Access to Services and Supports: Limited access to services and supports can be a significant barrier for individuals with autism and their families. These services may include therapies, interventions, medical care, and community resources. Barriers to access can be due to

factors such as geographical location, financial constraints, long waitlists, or inadequate service availability.

7. Stigma and Discrimination: Stigma and discrimination surrounding autism can create significant barriers for individuals with autism. They may face negative attitudes, stereotypes, and exclusion from social activities, employment opportunities, or educational settings. Stigma can contribute to feelings of shame, low self-esteem, and hinder their ability to fully participate in society.

By understanding these barriers, society can work towards creating a more inclusive and supportive environment for individuals with autism. It involves promoting awareness, providing necessary accommodations and supports, and challenging stigmatizing attitudes and practices. Breaking down these barriers is crucial in empowering individuals with autism to reach their full potential and lead fulfilling lives.

2. Overcoming Challenges:

Overcoming challenges is a vital aspect of the journey for individuals with autism. It involves developing strategies, acquiring skills, and seeking support to navigate and surpass obstacles. Here's a straightforward explanation of the process of overcoming challenges:

1. Identifying and Understanding Challenges: The first step in overcoming challenges is to identify and understand them. This includes recognizing the specific areas where individuals with autism face difficulties, such as communication, social interaction, sensory sensitivities, or academic tasks. Understanding these challenges provides a foundation for finding effective solutions.

2. Developing Individualized Strategies: Once challenges are identified, individuals with autism can develop individualized strategies to address them. These strategies may involve using visual supports, implementing structured routines, practicing social skills, or employing sensory regulation techniques. Tailoring strategies to individual strengths and needs increases their effectiveness.

3. Building Skills and Capacities: Overcoming challenges often requires building skills and capacities. This can involve working on communication skills, social interaction, sensory integration, executive functioning, and self-regulation abilities. Skill-building interventions, therapies, and educational supports can play a crucial role in enhancing these capabilities.

4. Seeking Support and Collaboration: Individuals with autism can benefit from seeking support and collaborating with professionals, educators, therapists, and support networks. These individuals can provide guidance, specialized interventions, and resources to help overcome challenges. Collaborating with others also fosters a sense of community and creates opportunities for learning and growth.

5. Encouraging Persistence and Resilience: Overcoming challenges requires persistence and resilience. Individuals with autism and their support systems need to foster a mindset of perseverance, embracing setbacks as learning

opportunities, and staying motivated to keep trying. Developing resilience helps individuals bounce back from difficulties and continue moving forward.

6. Celebrating Progress and Success: Recognizing and celebrating progress and success is essential in the journey of overcoming challenges. Even small achievements deserve acknowledgment and celebration, as they reinforce individuals' confidence, self-esteem, and motivation to continue their efforts. Celebrating progress provides a positive outlook and a sense of accomplishment.

By actively working to overcome challenges, individuals with autism can develop their skills, gain independence, and improve their overall quality of life. This process involves understanding the specific challenges, developing strategies, seeking support, fostering resilience, and acknowledging progress along the way.

3. Building Skills and Capacities:

Building skills and capacities is a fundamental aspect of the journey for individuals with autism. It involves developing and enhancing various abilities to overcome challenges and promote personal growth. Here's a direct explanation of building skills and capacities:

1. Communication Skills: Building communication skills is crucial for individuals with autism. This includes improving verbal and nonverbal communication, understanding social cues, expressing needs and emotions effectively, and engaging in meaningful conversations. Speech therapy, social skills training, and augmentative and alternative communication (AAC) systems can aid in developing these skills.

2. Social Interaction: Enhancing social interaction skills is important for individuals with autism to form and maintain relationships. This involves understanding social rules and norms, interpreting nonverbal cues, developing empathy, and engaging in reciprocal conversations. Social skills training, peer support programs, and structured social opportunities can assist in building these skills.

3. Sensory Regulation: Developing sensory regulation abilities helps individuals with autism manage sensory sensitivities and preferences. This includes techniques to cope with sensory overload, self-calming strategies, and adaptive responses to sensory stimuli. Occupational therapy and sensory integration interventions can provide support in developing sensory regulation skills.

4. Executive Functioning: Building executive functioning skills is essential for individuals with autism to manage tasks, plan, organize, and self-regulate behavior. This involves improving abilities such as attention, problem-solving, organization, time management, and flexibility. Cognitive behavioral therapy, visual supports, and structured routines can aid in developing executive functioning skills.

5. Independent Living Skills: Acquiring independent living skills enables individuals with autism to lead more autonomous lives. This includes tasks such as personal hygiene, household chores, money management, cooking,

and transportation skills. Life skills training, occupational therapy, and community-based programs can help develop these skills.

6. Academic Skills: Enhancing academic skills is important for individuals with autism to succeed in educational settings. This involves improving reading, writing, math, and study skills. Individualized educational plans (IEPs), specialized instruction, assistive technology, and educational support services can assist in building academic skills.

7. Emotional Regulation: Developing emotional regulation skills helps individuals with autism understand and manage their emotions effectively. This includes identifying emotions, coping with stress, practicing self-regulation techniques, and seeking support when needed. Therapy, mindfulness practices, and social-emotional learning programs can support the development of emotional regulation skills.

By actively building these skills and capacities, individuals with autism can enhance their abilities, increase independence, and improve their overall quality of life. It involves targeted interventions, therapies, educational supports, and practice in real-life situations.

4. Support Systems:

Support systems are essential networks of assistance and resources that provide guidance and aid to individuals with autism. They help individuals and their families navigate challenges and promote overall well-being. Here's a direct explanation of support systems:

1. Family Support: Families play a crucial role in providing love, understanding, and advocacy for individuals with autism. They offer emotional support, participate in therapies, and create a nurturing home environment.

2. Professional Support: Professionals such as therapists, educators, and medical practitioners provide specialized

interventions, assessments, and guidance tailored to the unique needs of individuals with autism.

3. Peer Support: Peer support groups and social skills training programs connect individuals with autism to others who share similar experiences, fostering friendships and providing opportunities for shared understanding.

4. Community Organizations: Autism-focused community organizations offer resources, workshops, and events that address various aspects of autism. They connect individuals and families with local services, support groups, and advocacy initiatives.

5. Educational Support: Schools and educational institutions provide individualized education plans (IEPs), accommodations, and specialized instruction to meet the unique learning needs of individuals with autism.

6. Government Programs: Government programs offer support in accessing services and resources, including

healthcare coverage, early intervention programs, disability benefits, and vocational rehabilitation services.

7. Online Communities: Online communities and forums provide virtual support, allowing individuals and families to share information, connect with others, and find support from those who understand the challenges of autism.

Having a robust support system, including family, professionals, peers, community organizations, educational institutions, government programs, and online communities, is crucial for individuals with autism to access resources, guidance, and emotional support. These networks contribute to overall well-being and success.

5. Persistence and Resilience:

Persistence and resilience are essential qualities for individuals with autism to navigate challenges, overcome obstacles, and achieve personal growth. Here's a concise explanation:

1. Persistence: Persistence refers to the ability to continue striving towards goals despite setbacks and difficulties. Individuals with autism often encounter obstacles in various areas of their lives, such as communication, social interaction, and academic tasks. By maintaining persistence, they can persevere through challenges, seek alternative solutions, and make progress towards their objectives.

2. Resilience: Resilience is the capacity to bounce back from adversity and adapt to changing circumstances. Individuals with autism may face barriers and setbacks that can impact their self-esteem and motivation. Resilience allows them to recover from setbacks, learn from experiences, and develop coping strategies to better navigate future challenges.

3. Problem-Solving Skills: Developing problem-solving skills is crucial for individuals with autism to overcome obstacles. It involves identifying problems, analyzing potential solutions, and implementing effective strategies. By honing their problem-solving abilities, individuals with

autism can approach challenges with a proactive and solution-oriented mindset.

4. Support Systems: Having a strong support system contributes to resilience. Family, friends, professionals, and community networks can offer emotional support, guidance, and practical assistance. Supportive relationships provide individuals with autism the resources and encouragement necessary to persist in the face of challenges.

5. Self-Advocacy: Building self-advocacy skills empowers individuals with autism to express their needs, communicate their strengths, and assert their rights. By advocating for themselves, they can overcome barriers, access necessary support, and create environments that accommodate their unique needs.

6. Mindset: Cultivating a positive mindset is crucial for persistence and resilience. Individuals with autism can develop a growth mindset, embracing challenges as opportunities for learning and growth. By focusing on

progress rather than perfection, they can maintain motivation and continue to develop their skills and capacities.

7. Celebrating Success: Recognizing and celebrating achievements, no matter how small, reinforces persistence and resilience. By acknowledging their progress, individuals with autism can build confidence, maintain motivation, and develop a positive outlook on their abilities and potential.

By fostering persistence and resilience, individuals with autism can navigate challenges, overcome barriers, and achieve personal goals. These qualities empower them to adapt to new situations, develop problem-solving skills, advocate for themselves, and celebrate their successes along the journey.

6. Celebrating Success:

Celebrating success is an important aspect of the journey for individuals with autism. It involves acknowledging and recognizing achievements, no matter how small, to reinforce confidence, motivation, and a positive self-perception. Here's a direct explanation of celebrating success:

1. Acknowledging Achievements: Celebrating success begins with acknowledging the accomplishments of individuals with autism. This includes recognizing progress made in various areas of their lives, such as communication, social skills, academic achievements, independent living skills, or personal growth. By acknowledging these achievements, individuals feel a sense of validation and encouragement.

2. Boosting Confidence: Celebrating success helps to boost confidence and self-esteem. By acknowledging their efforts and highlighting their strengths, individuals with autism gain a more positive perception of themselves and their abilities. This confidence serves as a foundation for continued growth and perseverance.

3. Motivation and Progress: Celebrating success fuels motivation. When individuals with autism see the positive outcomes of their efforts, they are more likely to stay motivated and continue striving towards their goals. Celebrating success provides a sense of accomplishment and satisfaction, reinforcing the desire to keep making progress.

4. Recognizing Effort: Celebrating success is not solely focused on the outcome but also recognizes the effort invested. Individuals with autism often face unique challenges that require extra effort to overcome. By acknowledging the hard work and determination they put into their endeavors, they feel valued and validated for their commitment.

5. Creating a Positive Outlook: Celebrating success fosters a positive outlook on life. It helps individuals with autism develop a mindset that focuses on their abilities, strengths, and the progress they have made. This positive perspective allows them to approach future challenges with optimism and resilience.

6. Social and Emotional Well-being: Celebrating success contributes to the social and emotional well-being of individuals with autism. It provides opportunities for connection, as others can join in celebrating their achievements. It also fosters a sense of pride and accomplishment, which positively impacts their overall mental and emotional health.

7. Cultivating a Supportive Environment: Celebrating success creates a supportive environment for individuals with autism. When family members, friends, teachers, and support networks actively participate in celebrating achievements, it reinforces a sense of community, belonging, and encouragement. This support system plays a crucial role in the ongoing journey of individuals with autism.

By actively celebrating success, individuals with autism experience increased confidence, motivation, and a positive outlook on their abilities. It creates a nurturing and supportive environment that fosters ongoing growth, development, and well-being.

By breaking through barriers, individuals with autism can develop their strengths, reach their potential, and lead fulfilling lives. It is a journey that requires perseverance, support, and the belief that barriers can be overcome. This section highlights the importance of recognizing and addressing barriers while fostering resilience and celebrating achievements along the way.

Chapter 3

The Power of Understanding

This Chapter addresses the importance of raising awareness, knowledge and empathy to promote acceptance and support for people with autism.

A direct description of comprehension is:

1. Sensitization:
Sensitization is a process that involves raising awareness and understanding about autism in order to foster empathy, acceptance, and support for individuals on the autism spectrum. Here's a direct explanation of sensitization:

1. Raising Awareness: Sensitization aims to increase public knowledge and understanding of autism. It involves sharing accurate information about the characteristics, strengths, and challenges associated with autism. By providing educational materials, organizing awareness campaigns, and engaging in community outreach,

sensitization efforts ensure that accurate information reaches a wide audience.

2. Dispelling Misconceptions: Sensitization challenges common misconceptions and stereotypes surrounding autism. It provides accurate and up-to-date information to counter misinformation or outdated beliefs. By dispelling misconceptions, sensitization helps create a more informed and accepting society.

3. Promoting Empathy: Sensitization seeks to foster empathy by encouraging individuals to put themselves in the shoes of someone with autism. This perspective-taking approach helps people understand the unique experiences and challenges faced by individuals on the autism spectrum. By promoting empathy, sensitization promotes a more compassionate and supportive attitude towards individuals with autism.

4. Encouraging Inclusion: Sensitization efforts aim to promote inclusive practices in various settings, such as schools, workplaces, and communities. By increasing

understanding about the diverse needs and strengths of individuals with autism, sensitization helps create environments that accommodate and embrace neurodiversity. It encourages the development of inclusive policies, programs, and initiatives that ensure equal opportunities and participation for individuals with autism.

5. Supporting Families and Caregivers: Sensitization recognizes the importance of supporting families and caregivers of individuals with autism. It provides resources, information, and emotional support to help them navigate the challenges they may encounter. By raising awareness about the needs of families and caregivers, sensitization fosters a more supportive and understanding community.

6. Advocacy: Sensitization encourages individuals to become advocates for individuals with autism. It empowers people to speak up, raise awareness, and promote positive change in policies, services, and attitudes towards autism. By advocating for inclusive practices and

policies, sensitization contributes to a more inclusive and accepting society.

7. Collaborative Efforts: Sensitization is most effective when it involves collaboration among various stakeholders, including individuals with autism, families, professionals, community organizations, and policymakers. By working together, these stakeholders can pool their resources, expertise, and experiences to create a comprehensive and impactful sensitization campaign.

Sensitization plays a crucial role in creating a more inclusive and accepting society for individuals with autism. By raising awareness, dispelling misconceptions, promoting empathy, encouraging inclusion, supporting families, and advocating for positive change, sensitization efforts contribute to a society that embraces and celebrates the unique contributions of individuals on the autism spectrum.

2. Empathy and Respect for Perspectives:

Empathy and respect for perspectives are fundamental qualities that foster understanding, acceptance, and support for individuals with autism. Here's a direct explanation:

1. Empathy: Empathy is the ability to understand and share the feelings and experiences of others. When it comes to individuals with autism, empathy plays a crucial role in building connections and fostering a supportive environment. By putting themselves in the shoes of individuals with autism, people can better understand their challenges, frustrations, and unique perspectives.

2. Understanding Diverse Perspectives: Autism is a spectrum disorder, and individuals on the spectrum have diverse experiences and perspectives. Respect for these perspectives means acknowledging and valuing the individuality of each person with autism. It involves recognizing that there is no single "autistic experience" and that each person's journey is unique.

3. Avoiding Judgment: Empathy and respect require avoiding judgment and preconceived notions about autism.

It means approaching individuals with autism with an open mind, free from biases or assumptions. By suspending judgment, people can better appreciate the individual strengths, capabilities, and potential of individuals with autism.

4. Active Listening: Active listening is a key component of empathy and respect. It involves genuinely hearing and understanding the thoughts, feelings, and concerns expressed by individuals with autism. Through active listening, people can validate their experiences, offer support, and build trusting relationships.

5. Validation and Acceptance: Empathy and respect involve validating the emotions and experiences of individuals with autism. It means acknowledging their challenges and frustrations without minimizing or dismissing them. By validating their experiences, people can foster a sense of acceptance and belonging for individuals with autism.

6. Supporting Communication Needs: Empathy and respect also encompass supporting the unique communication needs of individuals with autism. This may involve being patient, using clear and concise language, and employing alternative communication methods such as visual supports or assistive technologies. By adapting communication styles, people can ensure effective and respectful interactions.

7. Collaborative Decision-Making: Empathy and respect promote collaborative decision-making. It involves involving individuals with autism in decisions that affect their lives, such as educational plans, therapy options, or daily routines. By including their perspectives and preferences, people can ensure that individuals with autism have a voice and agency in their own lives.

By embracing empathy and respect for perspectives, individuals can create a more inclusive and supportive environment for individuals with autism. These qualities facilitate understanding, promote acceptance, and pave the way for meaningful connections and opportunities for individuals with autism to thrive.

3. Challenging stereotypes:

Challenging stereotypes involves questioning and dispelling commonly held misconceptions about individuals with autism. Here's a direct explanation:

1. Stereotypes about Abilities: Stereotypes often portray individuals with autism as lacking abilities or intelligence. Challenging these stereotypes means recognizing the diverse range of strengths and talents that individuals on the autism spectrum possess. It involves highlighting their unique abilities in areas such as pattern recognition, attention to detail, creativity, and problem-solving.

2. Social and Communication Skills: Stereotypes sometimes suggest that individuals with autism are socially withdrawn or incapable of meaningful communication. Challenging these stereotypes requires acknowledging that social and communication skills can vary among

individuals with autism. It involves recognizing that individuals with autism may have different ways of expressing themselves and may benefit from alternative communication methods. Challenging stereotypes means emphasizing the potential for individuals with autism to develop and maintain meaningful relationships.

3. Intellectual Abilities: Stereotypes may wrongly assume that individuals with autism have intellectual disabilities. Challenging these stereotypes involves recognizing that intelligence is not determined by autism alone. Individuals with autism can have a wide range of intellectual abilities, from average to above average IQ levels. Challenging stereotypes means acknowledging their potential for academic success and professional achievements.

4. Behavioral Challenges: Stereotypes may focus solely on challenging behaviors associated with autism, portraying individuals as disruptive or difficult to manage. Challenging these stereotypes requires understanding that challenging behaviors can stem from various factors, including sensory sensitivities, communication difficulties,

or anxiety. It involves recognizing that individuals with autism may need support and strategies to manage their behavior effectively.

5. Homogeneity of Autism: Stereotypes often present autism as a homogeneous condition, neglecting the vast diversity within the autism spectrum. Challenging these stereotypes means understanding that autism is a spectrum disorder, and individuals on the spectrum have unique experiences, strengths, and challenges. It involves appreciating the individuality and diversity of those on the autism spectrum.

6. Limitations in Employment: Stercotypes may falsely assume that individuals with autism are unable to succeed in the workplace. Challenging these stereotypes requires recognizing that individuals with autism can make valuable contributions in various industries. It involves promoting inclusive employment practices, providing accommodations, and highlighting success stories of individuals with autism in the workforce.

7. Potential for Growth and Development: Challenging stereotypes means acknowledging that individuals with autism have the potential for growth, learning, and personal development. It involves fostering environments that provide opportunities for individuals with autism to reach their full potential, pursue their interests, and lead fulfilling lives.

By challenging stereotypes, society can promote a more accurate and nuanced understanding of autism. This leads to increased acceptance, appreciation of individual strengths, and the creation of inclusive environments that empower individuals with autism to thrive and contribute to society.

4. Neurodiversity and acceptance:

Neurodiversity is a concept that recognizes and embraces the natural variations in neurological development, including autism. Acceptance, in the context of neurodiversity, involves valuing and respecting the diverse ways in which individuals' brains function. Here's a direct explanation:

1. Valuing Differences:

Neurodiversity and acceptance involve valuing the inherent differences in neurological development. Rather than viewing autism as a disorder that needs to be fixed or cured, this perspective emphasizes that neurological differences are a natural and valuable part of human diversity.

2. Shifting Perspectives: Acceptance challenges the notion that being neurotypical is the norm or ideal. It shifts the focus from attempting to make individuals with autism conform to neurotypical standards to embracing and accommodating their unique strengths, challenges, and perspectives.

3. Celebrating Strengths: Neurodiversity and acceptance recognize and celebrate the unique strengths and talents that individuals with autism bring. These strengths may include exceptional attention to detail, pattern recognition, creativity, and innovative problem-solving abilities.

Embracing these strengths promotes a more inclusive and appreciative view of individuals on the autism spectrum.

4. Embracing Accommodations: Acceptance involves providing accommodations that support the specific needs of individuals with autism. These accommodations may include sensory supports, communication tools, flexible learning environments, or workplace adjustments. By embracing and implementing accommodations, society can create inclusive spaces that allow individuals with autism to fully participate and thrive.

5. Respectful Language and Attitudes: Neurodiversity and acceptance promote the use of respectful language and attitudes when referring to individuals with autism. This means using person-first language, such as "person with autism," to emphasize the individual's identity beyond their diagnosis. It also involves avoiding derogatory or stigmatizing language that perpetuates negative stereotypes.

6. Advocacy and Inclusion: Embracing neurodiversity and acceptance involves advocating for inclusive practices and policies that promote equal opportunities for individuals with autism. This includes advocating for accessible education, employment, and community resources that accommodate the needs of individuals with autism and promote their full participation and inclusion.

7. Recognizing Potential and Contributions: Neurodiversity and acceptance recognize the potential of individuals with autism to make meaningful contributions to society. This perspective encourages the cultivation of environments that provide opportunities for individuals with autism to showcase their abilities, pursue their interests, and contribute their unique perspectives and talents to various domains.

By embracing neurodiversity and acceptance, society can foster a more inclusive and understanding environment for individuals with autism. This leads to increased appreciation of their strengths, opportunities for self-advocacy, and the creation of communities that value and celebrate the diversity of neurological experiences.

5. Advocacy and Support:

Advocacy and support are essential components in ensuring the well-being, rights, and inclusion of individuals with autism. Here's a direct explanation:

1. Amplifying Voices: Advocacy involves amplifying the voices of individuals with autism and empowering them to express their needs, preferences, and concerns. It means advocating for their rights to be heard and actively participating in decisions that affect their lives.

2. Access to Services: Advocacy includes ensuring individuals with autism have access to necessary services and supports. This may involve advocating for inclusive educational settings, appropriate therapies, medical care, and community resources that address their unique needs.

3. Navigating Systems: Advocacy provides support in navigating complex systems such as education, healthcare, and social services. It involves assisting individuals with autism and their families in understanding their rights, accessing available supports, and advocating for appropriate services.

4. Policy Change: Advocacy plays a crucial role in advocating for policy changes that promote the rights and inclusion of individuals with autism. This includes advocating for legislation that supports inclusive education, employment opportunities, healthcare coverage, and anti-discrimination measures.

5. Awareness and Education: Advocacy includes raising awareness about autism and promoting accurate understanding among the general public, policymakers, and professionals. It involves dispelling misconceptions, sharing personal stories, and providing educational resources to foster a more inclusive and accepting society.

6. Peer Support: Support for individuals with autism extends to creating peer support networks and communities. These networks provide a platform for individuals with autism to connect, share experiences, and provide mutual support. They play a vital role in reducing isolation, promoting self-advocacy, and fostering a sense of belonging.

7. Family Support: Advocacy and support extend to families of individuals with autism. It involves providing information, resources, and emotional support to families as they navigate the challenges and opportunities associated with raising a child with autism. Supporting families contributes to the overall well-being and success of individuals with autism.

Advocacy and support are instrumental in ensuring that individuals with autism have equal access to opportunities, rights, and a fulfilling life. By amplifying their voices, advocating for policy changes, providing access to services, raising awareness, and fostering support networks, advocates contribute to a more inclusive and empowering society for individuals with autism and their families.

6. Promote inclusion:

This chapter emphasizes the importance of building inclusive communities, schools and workplaces. By understanding the unique needs and strengths of people with autism, readers can take action to create an environment that promotes acceptance, respect and equal opportunity for people with autism to thrive. will be able to

7. Family and Community Support:

Understanding autism goes beyond individual perceptions and includes support for families and communities. This chapter emphasizes the importance of providing resources, services and emotional support to families of people with autism. Explore community initiatives and programs that promote inclusion and well-being. By harnessing the power of understanding, readers can become agents of positive change in the lives of people with autism. Through increased awareness, empathy and support, we can create a more inclusive and accepting society that values and celebrates the unique contributions of people on the autism spectrum.

Chapter 4

Embracing Neurodiversity

Embracing neurodiversity means recognizing and celebrating the natural variations in neurological development, including autism. It involves accepting and appreciating the unique strengths, perspectives, and contributions of individuals with diverse neurological profiles. Here's a direct explanation:

1. Appreciating Individuality:

Appreciating individuality is a core aspect of embracing neurodiversity and recognizing the unique qualities of individuals with autism. Here's the main point explained:

1. Recognizing Unique Strengths: Appreciating individuality involves recognizing and valuing the unique strengths that individuals with autism possess. These strengths can vary widely and may include exceptional attention to detail, heightened sensory perception,

exceptional memory, pattern recognition, creativity, and a strong focus on specific interests or topics. By acknowledging and celebrating these strengths, society can provide opportunities for individuals with autism to thrive in areas where they excel.

2. Acknowledging Diverse Challenges: Individuality also encompasses acknowledging and understanding the diverse challenges that individuals with autism may face. While autism is characterized by certain common challenges, such as difficulties with social interaction and communication, each individual's experience is unique. Some may struggle with sensory sensitivities, executive functioning, or managing anxiety. By recognizing these challenges and providing appropriate support and accommodations, we can help individuals with autism navigate their daily lives more effectively.

3. Respecting Preferences and Differences: Appreciating individuality means respecting the preferences and differences of individuals with autism. This includes understanding that they may have different communication

styles, sensory needs, or ways of interacting with the world. Respecting these differences involves creating inclusive environments that accommodate their specific needs and preferences, promoting self-expression, and fostering a sense of belonging.

4. Avoiding Stereotyping: Appreciating individuality requires avoiding generalizations and stereotypes about individuals with autism. It is crucial to recognize that each person's experience and abilities are unique and not to make assumptions based on preconceived notions. By avoiding stereotypes, we can create an environment that values and respects the diverse range of experiences and capabilities within the autism community.

5. Tailoring Support and Accommodations: Appreciating individuality emphasizes the importance of providing tailored support and accommodations to individuals with autism. Recognizing their unique strengths, challenges, and preferences helps inform the development of individualized strategies and interventions that can support their well-being and development. By taking an

individualized approach, we can provide the specific support needed to promote growth and success for each person.

6. Encouraging Self-Advocacy: Appreciating individuality involves empowering individuals with autism to advocate for themselves and their needs. It means supporting their self-advocacy efforts, helping them develop self-awareness and self-advocacy skills, and promoting their active participation in decision-making processes that affect their lives. By encouraging self-advocacy, we promote autonomy, self-determination, and the recognition of individual voices within the autism community.

Appreciating individuality is a fundamental aspect of embracing neurodiversity. By recognizing the unique strengths, challenges, preferences, and abilities of individuals with autism, we can foster an inclusive and supportive society that values and respects the individuality of each person.

2. Valuing Different Ways of Thinking:

Valuing different ways of thinking is an essential aspect of embracing neurodiversity and recognizing the diverse cognitive profiles of individuals with autism. Here's the main point explained:

1. Recognizing Cognitive Diversity: Valuing different ways of thinking involves recognizing that individuals with autism may have cognitive profiles that differ from neurotypical individuals. They may process information, perceive the world, and think in unique and alternative ways. Rather than viewing these differences as deficits, valuing cognitive diversity means appreciating the strengths and alternative perspectives that individuals with autism bring to the table.

2. Unique Problem-Solving Approaches: Individuals with autism often exhibit unique problem-solving abilities. They may excel at pattern recognition, attention to detail, logical reasoning, or thinking outside the box. Valuing different ways of thinking means acknowledging and appreciating these cognitive strengths. By embracing these unique problem-solving approaches, we can foster

innovation, creativity, and alternative solutions to complex challenges.

3. Diverse Learning Styles: Valuing different ways of thinking recognizes that individuals with autism may have diverse learning styles. They may benefit from visual supports, hands-on experiences, or structured learning environments. By embracing these diverse learning styles, we can provide educational opportunities that cater to the individual needs of learners with autism, ensuring their optimal engagement and understanding.

4. Alternative Perspectives: Individuals with autism often offer alternative perspectives that can provide valuable insights in various domains. Their distinct ways of perceiving and processing information can contribute fresh ideas, unique observations, and novel approaches to problem-solving. Valuing different ways of thinking means actively seeking out and considering these alternative perspectives, broadening our understanding and enhancing collective decision-making processes.

5. Fostering Collaboration: Valuing different ways of thinking promotes collaboration and teamwork that embraces diverse cognitive profiles, including autism. By bringing together individuals with different thinking styles and cognitive strengths, we create opportunities for collaborative problem-solving, mutual learning, and the development of well-rounded solutions. Collaborative environments that value different ways of thinking foster a culture of inclusivity, respect, and appreciation for diverse perspectives.

6. Redefining Intelligence: Valuing different ways of thinking challenges traditional notions of intelligence and recognizes that intelligence encompasses a wide range of abilities and cognitive profiles. It emphasizes that intelligence is not limited to a single measure or set of skills but can manifest in various ways. By embracing the diverse cognitive abilities of individuals with autism, we redefine and expand our understanding of intelligence.

By valuing different ways of thinking, society can create inclusive environments that celebrate cognitive diversity, foster innovation, and promote the inclusion and empowerment of individuals with autism. Recognizing and appreciating the unique cognitive strengths, learning styles, problem-solving approaches, and alternative perspectives of individuals with autism contributes to a more enriched and diverse society as a whole.

3. Promoting Inclusion:

Promoting inclusion is a key aspect of embracing neurodiversity and ensuring that individuals with autism are valued, respected, and fully integrated into all aspects of society. Here's the main point explained:

1. Equal Opportunities: Promoting inclusion means providing individuals with autism equal opportunities to participate and engage in all areas of life, including education, employment, social interactions, and community involvement. It involves removing barriers and creating environments that accommodate their unique needs and abilities, ensuring that they have access to the same opportunities as their neurotypical peers.

2. Accessibility and Accommodations: Promoting inclusion requires making environments and activities accessible to individuals with autism. This includes providing accommodations such as visual supports, sensory-friendly spaces, alternative communication methods, and assistive technologies. By ensuring accessibility, we enable individuals with autism to fully participate and contribute in various settings, allowing them to reach their full potential.

3. Inclusive Education: Promoting inclusion in education involves creating inclusive learning environments that cater to the diverse needs of students with autism. It includes providing necessary supports, individualized education plans, and specialized teaching strategies that facilitate their learning and social development. Inclusive education fosters acceptance, understanding, and positive relationships among students of all abilities.

4. Employment Opportunities: Promoting inclusion in the workplace means ensuring that individuals with autism

have access to meaningful employment opportunities. It involves creating inclusive hiring practices, providing reasonable accommodations, and offering supportive work environments that value diversity and recognize the unique strengths and contributions of individuals with autism. Inclusive employment promotes financial independence, self-esteem, and social integration.

5. Social Integration: Promoting inclusion entails facilitating social integration for individuals with autism. This includes creating opportunities for social interaction, fostering peer relationships, and promoting community engagement. It involves raising awareness and understanding among the general public about autism, combating stigma, and creating accepting and inclusive communities where individuals with autism can participate and belong.

6. Advocacy and Support: Promoting inclusion requires advocating for the rights and needs of individuals with autism. It involves promoting inclusive policies, influencing systemic change, and ensuring that appropriate

supports and services are available. Advocacy and support empower individuals with autism and their families to navigate systems, access resources, and assert their rights, enabling them to fully participate in society.

7. Cultural Shift: Promoting inclusion necessitates a cultural shift in attitudes and perceptions towards autism. It involves challenging stereotypes, dispelling misconceptions, and promoting acceptance and understanding. By fostering a culture that values diversity and embraces neurodiversity, we create a society that is inclusive, supportive, and respectful of the rights and dignity of individuals with autism.

Promoting inclusion is crucial for creating a society that values and respects the rights and contributions of individuals with autism. By ensuring equal opportunities, providing accommodations, fostering inclusive education and employment, facilitating social integration, advocating for support, and driving cultural change, we can build a more inclusive and equitable world for individuals with autism to thrive and participate fully in all aspects of life.

4. Challenging Stereotypes:

Challenging stereotypes is an important aspect of embracing neurodiversity and promoting a more accurate and nuanced understanding of individuals with autism. Here's the main point explained:

1. Dispelling Misconceptions: Challenging stereotypes involves dispelling misconceptions and correcting inaccurate beliefs about individuals with autism. It requires providing accurate information about autism and debunking common myths that contribute to misunderstanding and stigmatization. By challenging misconceptions, we can promote a more informed and empathetic view of autism.

2. Recognizing Individuality: Challenging stereotypes means recognizing that individuals with autism are unique individuals with diverse strengths, challenges, and experiences. It rejects the notion of a homogeneous "autistic" identity and emphasizes the importance of understanding and appreciating each person's individuality.

By recognizing individuality, we avoid generalizations and acknowledge the wide range of abilities and characteristics within the autism spectrum.

3. Highlighting Strengths: Challenging stereotypes involves highlighting the strengths and positive qualities of individuals with autism. While autism may present challenges in certain areas, individuals with autism also possess unique strengths and talents. By focusing on their abilities, such as attention to detail, analytical thinking, creativity, and specialized interests, we can challenge the notion that autism is solely a deficit or limitation.

4. Promoting Inclusive Language: Challenging stereotypes includes promoting the use of inclusive and respectful language when referring to individuals with autism. It encourages using person-first language, such as "individual with autism," to emphasize their personhood rather than defining them solely by their diagnosis. This promotes a more respectful and person-centered approach that acknowledges the complexity and diversity of their identities.

5. Emphasizing Potential and Growth: Challenging stereotypes involves emphasizing the potential for growth, development, and achievement among individuals with autism. It recognizes that with appropriate support, accommodations, and opportunities, individuals with autism can thrive and make significant contributions in various domains of life, including education, employment, and personal relationships. By highlighting their potential, we challenge the stereotype that individuals with autism are destined to be limited or dependent.

6. Encouraging Empathy and Understanding: Challenging stereotypes promotes empathy and understanding towards individuals with autism. It encourages society to recognize the unique challenges they may face in areas such as social interaction, communication, and sensory processing. By fostering empathy, we can create a more inclusive and supportive environment that embraces the diverse needs and experiences of individuals with autism.

7. Amplifying Authentic Voices: Challenging stereotypes involves amplifying the voices and experiences of individuals with autism themselves. It recognizes that they are the true experts in their own lives and encourages their active participation in shaping narratives, policies, and support systems. By listening to and valuing their perspectives, we challenge the notion that others can speak on their behalf or make assumptions about their experiences.

Challenging stereotypes is essential for fostering a more accurate and respectful understanding of individuals with autism. By dispelling misconceptions, recognizing individuality, highlighting strengths, promoting inclusive language, emphasizing potential and growth, encouraging empathy, and amplifying authentic voices, we can challenge stereotypes and create a society that embraces the diversity and richness of the autism community.

5. Fostering Collaboration and Mutual Learning: Fostering collaboration and mutual learning is a vital aspect of embracing neurodiversity and creating inclusive

environments that value the contributions and perspectives of individuals with autism. Here's the main point explained:

1. Recognizing Diverse Perspectives: Fostering collaboration and mutual learning involves recognizing and valuing the diverse perspectives that individuals with autism bring to the table. Their unique ways of thinking, problem-solving, and perceiving the world can offer fresh insights and alternative approaches to challenges. By acknowledging and respecting these diverse perspectives, we create opportunities for mutual learning and growth.

2. Creating Inclusive Spaces: Fostering collaboration means creating inclusive spaces where individuals with autism feel welcome, respected, and valued. This includes providing supportive environments that accommodate their sensory needs, communication styles, and social preferences. By creating inclusive spaces, we promote equal participation and active engagement, allowing for meaningful collaboration and mutual learning to take place.

3. Building Interdisciplinary Teams: Fostering collaboration involves building interdisciplinary teams that bring together individuals with diverse backgrounds, expertise, and perspectives, including those with autism. By creating teams that encompass a range of skills, knowledge, and experiences, we can leverage the strengths and contributions of each team member, fostering a collaborative environment where everyone's input is valued.

4. Promoting Active Listening and Respectful Dialogue: Fostering collaboration requires promoting active listening and respectful dialogue among team members. This involves creating an environment where everyone's ideas and opinions are heard and considered without judgment. By practicing active listening and respectful dialogue, we create a culture of open-mindedness, empathy, and mutual understanding, allowing for meaningful collaboration to flourish.

5. Sharing Knowledge and Experiences: Fostering collaboration and mutual learning involves sharing knowledge and experiences among team members, including individuals with autism. It means recognizing that everyone has unique expertise and insights to contribute. By sharing knowledge, experiences, and best practices, we create opportunities for mutual learning and professional development, enhancing the collective capabilities of the team.

6. Capitalizing on Strengths and Complementary Skills: Fostering collaboration means capitalizing on the strengths and complementary skills of team members, including those with autism. It involves recognizing and leveraging the unique talents, abilities, and perspectives of each individual, promoting a cooperative approach where everyone's strengths are valued and utilized. By capitalizing on strengths, we maximize the collective potential of the team.

7. Encouraging Growth and Personal Development: Fostering collaboration and mutual learning entails

creating an environment that encourages growth and personal development for all team members. It involves providing opportunities for learning, skill-building, and professional growth, recognizing that collaboration is not only about achieving specific goals but also about individual and collective growth.

Fostering collaboration and mutual learning among individuals with and without autism is essential for creating inclusive and innovative environments. By recognizing diverse perspectives, creating inclusive spaces, building interdisciplinary teams, promoting active listening and respectful dialogue, sharing knowledge and experiences, capitalizing on strengths, and encouraging growth and personal development, we foster a collaborative culture where all individuals can contribute, learn from one another, and achieve shared goals.

6. Advocating for Rights and Support:
Advocating for rights and support is a crucial aspect of embracing neurodiversity and ensuring that individuals with autism have access to the necessary resources,

services, and opportunities to thrive. Here's the main point explained:

1. Ensuring Equal Rights: Advocating for rights involves advocating for the equal rights and inclusion of individuals with autism in all areas of life. This includes advocating for access to education, employment, healthcare, housing, and community participation. By advocating for equal rights, we strive to eliminate discrimination, stigma, and barriers that may hinder the full participation and integration of individuals with autism in society.

2. Access to Quality Support: Advocating for support entails ensuring that individuals with autism have access to quality support services that meet their unique needs. This includes advocating for early intervention programs, specialized therapies, educational accommodations, and employment support. By advocating for comprehensive and individualized support, we aim to enhance the well-being, development, and independence of individuals with autism.

3. Empowering Self-Advocacy: Advocating for rights and support involves empowering individuals with autism to become self-advocates. This means supporting and equipping them with the necessary skills, knowledge, and resources to speak up for their rights, express their needs and preferences, and actively participate in decision-making processes that affect their lives. By fostering self-advocacy, we promote autonomy, self-determination, and empowerment.

4. Influencing Policies and Legislation: Advocating for rights and support requires influencing policies and legislation at local, national, and international levels. This includes advocating for the implementation of inclusive policies, funding for support services, and the development of legislation that protects the rights of individuals with autism. By influencing policies and legislation, we strive to create systemic change that supports the needs and rights of individuals with autism.

5. Raising Awareness and Changing Perceptions: Advocating for rights involves raising awareness and

changing societal perceptions about autism. This includes challenging stereotypes, dispelling myths, and promoting a more accurate and positive understanding of autism. By raising awareness, we seek to foster acceptance, understanding, and inclusion, creating a society that values and respects the rights and contributions of individuals with autism.

6. Collaboration and Coalition-Building: Advocating for rights and support often involves collaboration and coalition-building with other advocacy groups, organizations, and stakeholders. By forming alliances and working together, we amplify our collective voice, increase our impact, and create a united front in advocating for the rights and support of individuals with autism. Collaboration enables us to pool resources, share knowledge, and advocate more effectively for systemic change.

7. Addressing Intersectional Needs:
Advocating for rights and support requires addressing the intersectional needs of individuals with autism. This

includes considering how factors such as gender, race, ethnicity, socioeconomic status, and other identities intersect with autism and influence the experiences and challenges faced by individuals. By addressing intersectional needs, we strive for a more inclusive and equitable advocacy approach that recognizes and responds to the diverse experiences within the autism community.

Advocating for rights and support is essential for creating a society that respects, supports, and includes individuals with autism. By ensuring equal rights, access to quality support, empowering self-advocacy, influencing policies, raising awareness, fostering collaboration, and addressing intersectional needs, we can work towards a more inclusive and supportive environment where individuals with autism can thrive and fully participate in all aspects of life.

7. Shifting the Narrative: Embracing neurodiversity aims to shift the narrative around autism from a deficit-based model to one that focuses on strengths and potential. It encourages society to view autism as a natural variation

rather than a pathology, emphasizing the positive aspects and unique contributions that individuals with autism bring to the world.

By embracing neurodiversity, society can create a more inclusive, understanding, and supportive environment that values the diversity of neurological profiles, including autism. Embracing neurodiversity opens doors to opportunities, celebrates individuality, and fosters a more accepting and inclusive society for individuals with autism.

Chapter 5:

Unlocking the Solution

This Chapter focuses on unlocking the solution to effectively support individuals with autism and promote their overall well-being. It delves into the main strategies, approaches, and interventions that can help unlock the potential of individuals with autism. Here's the main point explained:

1. Person-Centered Approaches:
Person-centered approaches are fundamental in providing effective support and care for individuals with autism. These approaches prioritize the individual's unique needs, preferences, and goals, placing them at the center of decision-making and planning. The main point of person-centered approaches can be explained as follows:

1. Individualized Care: Person-centered approaches recognize that each individual with autism is unique, with their own set of strengths, challenges, and aspirations. The

main focus is on tailoring care and support to meet the specific needs and goals of the individual. This involves taking into account their interests, abilities, communication styles, and personal preferences to create a customized plan that maximizes their well-being and promotes their overall development.

2. Active Participation: Person-centered approaches emphasize the active participation of individuals with autism in decision-making processes. It involves engaging them as partners in their own care and support, allowing them to express their opinions, make choices, and have control over the decisions that affect their lives. This fosters a sense of empowerment, autonomy, and self-determination, promoting their confidence and self-esteem.

3. Respect for Autonomy: Person-centered approaches respect the autonomy and individuality of individuals with autism. This means valuing their personal choices, values, and beliefs, even if they differ from societal norms or expectations. It involves recognizing and honoring their right to make decisions about their own lives, while

providing the necessary support and guidance to ensure their well-being and safety.

4. Collaboration and Communication: Person-centered approaches promote collaboration and open communication between individuals with autism, their families, caregivers, and professionals. It recognizes that everyone involved has valuable insights and perspectives to contribute. By actively listening, valuing different viewpoints, and working together as a team, a comprehensive and holistic approach to care and support can be achieved.

5. Strengths-Based Focus: Person-centered approaches emphasize identifying and building upon the strengths and abilities of individuals with autism. Instead of solely focusing on deficits and challenges, these approaches seek to recognize and nurture their unique talents, interests, and capabilities. By harnessing their strengths, individuals can develop a sense of competence, achievement, and self-worth, leading to greater motivation and well-being.

6. Flexibility and Adaptability: Person-centered approaches recognize that the needs and goals of individuals with autism may change over time. They prioritize flexibility and adaptability in the care and support provided. This means being responsive to the individual's evolving needs, adjusting strategies as necessary, and continually reassessing progress. By being flexible and adaptable, person-centered approaches can effectively meet the changing requirements of individuals with autism.

7. Empathy and Compassion: Person-centered approaches foster an environment of empathy and compassion. They promote a deep understanding and acceptance of the individual's experiences, emotions, and challenges. This involves considering their feelings, providing emotional support, and creating a safe and nurturing space where they feel understood and valued.

Person-centered approaches are essential in ensuring that individuals with autism receive the support and care that best aligns with their unique needs and aspirations. By providing individualized care, fostering active participation, respecting autonomy, promoting collaboration, focusing on strengths, being flexible and adaptable, and cultivating empathy and compassion, these approaches empower individuals with autism to lead fulfilling and meaningful lives.

2. Individualized Education and Support: Individualized education and support are key elements in unlocking the potential of people with autism. It is about tailoring educational strategies, interventions and support services to meet each individual's unique needs, abilities and goals. The core of personalized education and support can be explained as follows.

1. Personalized learning:
Individualized education and support recognizes that people with autism have different learning styles, strengths and challenges. The main focus is to create a personalized study plan that addresses each individual's specific needs. This may include adapting teaching methods, materials

and classroom environments to meet the learning needs of our students and optimizing their educational experience.

2. Targeted interventions:
Personalized education and support includes the implementation of targeted interventions that address specific problem areas in people with autism. These interventions may include speech therapy, occupational therapy, social skills training, and behavioral interventions. By identifying each individual's unique needs and challenges, we can customize interventions to promote skill development, independence and overall well-being.

3. Adjustments and Changes:
Individualized education and support ensure appropriate consideration and adjustment for people with autism. This may include adjusting the learning environment such as visual supports, sensory breaks and assistive technology to improve access and participation. Adaptation and modification are aimed at removing barriers and creating an inclusive learning environment that supports individual success.

4. Cooperative Teamwork:

Personalized education and support requires the collaboration of educators, professionals, families and people with autism. This collaborative approach allows us to develop a holistic understanding of each individual's strengths, challenges and goals. Through collaboration, sharing of information and insights, we can build a comprehensive support system that maximizes individual educational opportunities and outcomes.

5. Monitoring and evaluating progress:

Individual education and support requires ongoing progress monitoring and assessment to assess intervention effectiveness and make necessary adjustments. Regular assessment of an individual's performance, progress and well-being helps identify areas for improvement and provides the basis for changes in educational strategies and support plans. This ensures that an individual's educational experience is always tailored to their evolving needs.

6. Transition plan:

Personalized education and support includes transition planning to support people with autism through important life transitions such as: B. Transition from early intervention to school, transition from school to post-secondary education or employment, or transition to independent living. Migration planning is the preparation of individuals for the new environment and expectations by identifying the supports, services and skills needed for a successful migration.

7. Family Promise:

Individual Education and Support recognizes the importance of including family members in educational activities for people with autism. This includes establishing open lines of communication, providing resources and information, and working with families to ensure consistent support and continuity of care. Involving the family makes the educational experience more holistic and integrated, promoting the overall well-being of the individual.

Personalized education and support enables people with autism to receive customized educational strategies, interventions and support services that address their individual needs and promote optimal development. individualize by providing individualized learning, targeted interventions, adjustments and modifications, encouraging collaborative teamwork, monitoring progress, facilitating smooth transitions, and engaging families. Good education and support enable people with autism to grow academically, socially and emotionally.

3. Applied Behavior Analysis (ABA):

Applied Behavior Analysis (ABA) is a scientific approach that focuses on understanding and modifying behavior to improve the lives of individuals with autism. It is based on the principles of learning theory and emphasizes the use of evidence-based strategies to address a wide range of behaviors and skill deficits. The main point of Applied Behavior Analysis can be explained as follows:

1. Behavior Modification: ABA aims to modify behavior by systematically analyzing and understanding the factors

that influence it. It involves breaking down complex behaviors into smaller, measurable units and using data-driven techniques to track progress. By identifying the antecedents (triggers) and consequences (reinforcers) of behavior, ABA practitioners can develop targeted interventions to increase desirable behaviors and decrease problematic ones.

2. Functional Assessment: ABA relies on conducting functional assessments to determine the underlying function or purpose of a behavior. This involves analyzing the environmental variables that influence behavior, such as the need for attention, escape from a demand, or access to a desired item. By understanding the function of behavior, ABA practitioners can develop individualized behavior intervention plans that effectively address the underlying causes.

3. Evidence-Based Interventions: ABA interventions are based on scientific research and evidence. ABA practitioners use a variety of techniques, such as positive reinforcement, prompting, shaping, and fading, to teach

new skills and modify behavior. These interventions are tailored to the individual's needs and are continuously evaluated and adjusted based on data analysis to ensure effectiveness.

4. Skill Acquisition: ABA focuses on teaching individuals with autism a wide range of skills, including communication, social interaction, daily living skills, academic skills, and self-management skills. ABA uses systematic instruction techniques to break down skills into smaller, manageable steps and gradually build up to more complex behaviors. Positive reinforcement is often used to motivate and reinforce desired skills, making learning a positive and engaging experience.

5. Behavior Reduction: ABA also addresses challenging behaviors by using techniques to decrease or eliminate them. This involves identifying the functions of the behaviors and implementing behavior intervention plans that provide alternative, more appropriate behaviors to replace problematic ones. ABA practitioners use strategies such as extinction (withholding reinforcement for

undesirable behaviors), punishment (applying consequences to decrease the frequency of a behavior), and functional communication training (teaching alternative communication methods).

6. Generalization and Maintenance: ABA emphasizes the generalization and maintenance of skills across different settings, people, and contexts. ABA practitioners strive to ensure that the skills learned in one environment or with one person transfer to other relevant situations. This is achieved through systematic programming, ongoing practice, and teaching individuals to use skills in various real-life situations.

7. Collaboration and Family Involvement: ABA recognizes the importance of collaboration and family involvement in the intervention process. ABA practitioners work closely with families, educators, and other professionals to develop consistent strategies and support plans. They provide training and guidance to caregivers, empowering them to implement behavior intervention techniques and

support the individual's progress outside of formal therapy sessions.

Applied Behavior Analysis is a widely recognized and extensively researched approach for addressing behavior and skill deficits in individuals with autism. By focusing on behavior modification, conducting functional assessments, using evidence-based interventions, promoting skill acquisition, reducing challenging behaviors, emphasizing generalization and maintenance, and fostering collaboration and family involvement, ABA aims to improve the overall quality of life for individuals with autism and help them reach their fullest potential.

4. Communication and Social Skills Development: Unlocking the solution includes prioritizing the development of communication and social skills for individuals with autism. Communication interventions, such as speech therapy, augmentative and alternative communication (AAC) systems, and social skills training, can help individuals improve their ability to express themselves, understand others, and navigate social

interactions. By focusing on communication and social skills development, we enhance their ability to connect with others and engage meaningfully in social contexts.

5. Sensory Integration and Regulation: Unlocking the solution involves addressing sensory integration and regulation challenges experienced by individuals with autism. Sensory-based interventions, such as sensory integration therapy and sensory diets, can help individuals better process and regulate sensory information. By creating sensory-friendly environments and providing strategies for self-regulation, we can support individuals in managing sensory sensitivities and promoting their overall well-being.

6. Assistive Technology and Accommodations: Unlocking the solution may require the use of assistive technology and accommodations to support individuals with autism. This can include visual supports, adaptive equipment, assistive communication devices, and technological tools that enhance independence, communication, and participation. By providing appropriate assistive

technology and accommodations, we empower individuals to overcome barriers and engage fully in various aspects of their lives.

7. Collaborative Teamwork: Unlocking the solution involves fostering collaborative teamwork among professionals, caregivers, and individuals with autism. This interdisciplinary collaboration ensures a holistic and coordinated approach to support. By working together, sharing expertise, and exchanging information, we can develop comprehensive and effective strategies that address the diverse needs of individuals with autism.

8. Lifelong Learning and Support: Unlocking the solution recognizes that support for individuals with autism is an ongoing process throughout their lifespan. It emphasizes the importance of lifelong learning, continued skill development, and ongoing support to adapt to new challenges and transitions. By providing lifelong learning opportunities and ongoing support, we enable individuals with autism to continually grow, achieve their goals, and lead meaningful lives.

Unlocking the solution requires a comprehensive, person-centered, and collaborative approach that addresses the unique needs and strengths of individuals with autism. By adopting individualized approaches, focusing on education and support, incorporating evidence-based interventions, promoting communication and social skills, addressing sensory challenges, providing assistive technology and accommodations, fostering collaborative teamwork, and emphasizing lifelong learning and support, we can unlock the potential of individuals with autism and support their overall well-being.

Chapter 6

A Future of Empowerment

The main point of this Chapter is to highlight the potential for individuals with autism to lead empowered and fulfilling lives. This chapter focuses on the strategies, initiatives, and societal changes necessary to create a future that embraces and supports neurodiversity, promotes inclusion, and ensures the rights and well-being of individuals with autism. The main points of this chapter can be explained as follows:

1. Shifting Paradigms:

The main point of the 'paradigm shift' section of this chapter is to emphasize the need to change society's perceptions and attitudes towards autism. It requires a paradigm shift from viewing autism as a defect or disability to recognizing and accepting it as a natural and valuable part of human diversity. The main points related to the paradigm shift can be explained as follows.

1. Embrace neurodiversity:

This chapter focuses on the concept of neurodiversity, which recognizes that neurological differences, including autism, are human neurological differences and not deviations from the norm. This promotes the idea that neurodiverse people, including those with autism, have unique strengths, perspectives and contributions they can offer to society.

2. Understanding Different Mindsets:

A paradigm shift requires understanding and appreciating the different ways of thinking and processing displayed by people with autism. This challenges the notion that there is only one "right" or "normal" way of thinking and promotes a broader understanding and acceptance of different cognitive styles.

3. Exceed deficit-based models.

This chapter criticizes deficit-based models that focus solely on the challenges and difficulties associated with autism. It advocates a more balanced perspective that recognizes and develops the strengths and capabilities of autistic people, rather than focusing on their shortcomings.

4. Challenging Prejudices and Stereotypes:

A paradigm shift means challenging the prejudices and stereotypes surrounding autism. The aim is to combat the misconceptions, prejudices and discriminatory attitudes that can marginalize people with autism. By disseminating accurate information and dispelling myths, society can create a more inclusive and accepting environment.

5. Empowering Autistic Voices:

A paradigm shift requires actively seeking out and amplifying the voices and experiences of people with autism. Recognize the importance of listening to and learning from people with autism themselves, as they provide unique insights, perspectives and expertise on autism-related issues doing.

6. Promote inclusivity and acceptance:

A paradigm shift requires promoting the inclusion and acceptance of people with autism in all areas. Encourage the creation of inclusive environments in schools, workplaces and communities where people with autism are accepted, valued and given equal opportunity to grow.

7. Protection of Rights and Precautions:
At Shifting Paradigms, we recognize the rights of people with autism and the importance of advocating for their access to adequate housing and support services. It calls for equal opportunity, reasonable accommodation, and the removal of barriers that prevent people with autism from participating fully in society.

Through a paradigm shift and a more inclusive and accepting view of autism, society can create a more supportive and empowering environment for people with autism. This will encourage a shift from a deficit-based perspective to one that recognizes and appreciates the unique strengths, abilities and contributions of people with autism, ultimately making it more inclusive and equitable for all. promote a brighter future.

2. Education and Employment Opportunities:

The main point of the Education and Employment Opportunities chapter section is to emphasize the importance of providing inclusive and equitable opportunities for people with autism in both education and employment. It highlights the need for customized approaches that address the unique strengths and challenges of people with autism and promote a society that values and supports their educational and career aspirations. The main points regarding education and employment opportunities can be explained as follows.

1. Inclusive education:

This chapter emphasizes the importance of inclusive education, ensuring that people with autism receive quality education alongside their neurotypical peers. We promote the idea of creating an inclusive learning environment that respects different learning styles and provides appropriate support to meet individual needs. Inclusive education helps promote social inclusion, academic growth and development of essential skills.

2. Personal Study Plan:

This chapter emphasizes the importance of recognizing the diverse learning needs of people with autism and developing individualized learning plans. These plans consider each individual's strengths, interests, and challenges and provide individualized strategies and arrangements to facilitate educational progress. Individualized learning plans help people with autism succeed in school and reach their full potential.

3. Vocational training and transition programs:

This chapter emphasizes the need for vocational training and transition programs that provide people with autism with the skills and knowledge they need to find employment. The focus of these programs is on developing work-specific skills, social and communication skills, and the ability to live independently. It also provides opportunities for people with autism to explore different career paths, gain work experience and facilitate a smooth transition into the world of work.

4. Workplace accommodation and support:

This chapter addresses the importance of creating inclusive workplaces that meet the unique needs of people with autism. This highlights the importance of providing reasonable accommodation in the workplace that: B. Sensory support, flexible schedules, and clear communication strategies to foster success in the workplace. Additionally, fostering a supportive work environment that promotes understanding, acceptance and diversity can help people with autism succeed in their chosen careers.

5. Entrepreneurship and self-employment:

This chapter recognizes the potential for individuals with autism to pursue entrepreneurship and self-employment as viable career options. Encourage the development of entrepreneurial skills, the provision of relevant training and resources, and the creation of support networks and mentoring programs to help people with autism start and run their own businesses.

6. Working with Employers and Educators:

This chapter emphasizes the importance of employers and educators working together to bridge the gap between the education and employment of people with autism. Promote awareness of autism in the workplace, provide training opportunities for employers, and foster partnerships that facilitate the transition of people with autism from school to work.

7. Standing up for equal opportunity:
This chapter emphasizes the need for lobbying to ensure equal opportunities in education and employment for people with autism. It calls for the implementation of policies and practices that prevent discrimination and promote inclusiveness, and the provision of comprehensive support services, job coaching and mentoring programs to facilitate integration into the world of work.

Prioritize inclusive education, provide individualized study plans, provide vocational training and transition programs, place people with autism in the workplace, encourage entrepreneurship and cooperation between employers and educators. By encouraging and advocating for equal opportunities, society can create environments in which people with autism feel safe to work. People with autism have the opportunity to survive, progress academically, and succeed in meaningful work.

3. Self-Advocacy and Empowerment:

The main points of the Self-advocacy and Empowerment section of this chapter are to develop self-advocacy skills so that people with autism can play an active role in advocating for their rights, needs, and desires. to emphasize the importance of It should promote self-determination, self-confidence, and autonomy in people with autism, enabling them to make choices, express their preferences, and actively participate in shaping their lives. emphasizes sexuality. The key points related to self-advocacy and empowerment can be explained as follows.

1. Self-determination and decision-making:

This chapter emphasizes the importance of promoting self-determination in people with autism. The organization recognizes the importance of empowering individuals to make decisions that affect their lives, including education, employment, relationships and overall well-being. By promoting self-determination, people with autism gain a sense of control and ownership of their lives.

2. Build your assertiveness skills.

This chapter emphasizes the need for people with autism to develop assertiveness skills. This includes developing effective communication strategies, self-expression techniques, and the ability to articulate needs, preferences and rights. Developing assertiveness skills enables people with autism to effectively assert themselves and voice their opinions and concerns.

3. Boost your confidence:

This chapter focuses on building self-confidence in people with autism. It provides support, encouragement, and opportunities to recognize potential challenges that individuals with autism may face during social interaction, public speaking, or self-expression, and to build confidence. emphasizing the importance of doing By developing self-confidence, people with autism are better able to assert themselves and defend their rights and needs.

4. Information and education:

This chapter emphasizes the importance of providing people with autism and their families with accurate information and education about autism-related issues, rights and resources. Accessible information helps people with autism understand their strengths, challenges, and rights so they can defend themselves effectively. It also enables them to make informed decisions about education, health care, and other aspects of life.

5. Create a supportive environment.

This chapter focuses on their role in creating a supportive environment that encourages self-expression and self-determination. This includes fostering inclusive and inclusive communities, schools, workplaces and social networks where people with autism are valued, respected and encouraged to express their views and needs. increase. Supportive environments provide opportunities for people with autism to practice assertiveness skills and receive support when needed.

6. Cooperation with Allies:

This chapter recognizes the importance of working with allies, including families, educators, medical professionals and advocacy groups, in supporting self-advocacy and self-determination. Encourage the development of partnerships that provide advice, guidance and resources to help people with autism navigate systems, access services and assert themselves effectively.

7. Assess individual strengths and contributions:

This chapter focuses on recognizing the individual strengths and contributions of people with autism. By recognizing and valuing the unique perspectives, talents, and abilities of people with autism, society can help them embrace their identities and speak confidently about their needs and aspirations. environment can be created.

By promoting self-assertion and self-determination, people with autism gain the skills, confidence and support they need to actively participate in the decision-making process, defend their rights, and live independently. Earn. This allows them to have a say, exercise choice and make meaningful contributions to their communities, thereby promoting a more inclusive and just society.

4. Supportive Communities and Networks:

The main point of the chapter section on "Supportive Communities and Networks" is to emphasize the importance of creating and fostering communities and networks that provide social support, understanding, and acceptance for individuals with autism. It highlights the significant role that supportive communities and networks play in enhancing the well-being, inclusion, and quality of life of individuals with autism. The main points related to supportive communities and networks can be explained as follows:

1. Building Connections and Relationships: The chapter emphasizes the importance of building connections and relationships within supportive communities and networks. It recognizes that individuals with autism thrive in

environments where they feel a sense of belonging and have opportunities to form meaningful relationships with peers, mentors, and allies. Building connections helps reduce social isolation and provides a support system for individuals with autism and their families.

2. Providing Emotional Support: Supportive communities and networks offer emotional support to individuals with autism and their families. This includes creating spaces where individuals with autism can express their emotions, share their experiences, and receive understanding and empathy. Emotional support helps individuals with autism navigate challenges, cope with stress, and develop resilience.

3. Sharing Knowledge and Information: Supportive communities and networks serve as platforms for sharing knowledge and information about autism-related topics, resources, and strategies. They provide opportunities for individuals with autism and their families to access information, learn from one another, and stay updated on

advancements in the field. Sharing knowledge promotes empowerment and informed decision-making.

4. Promoting Acceptance and Understanding: Supportive communities and networks promote acceptance and understanding of individuals with autism. They challenge stereotypes, educate others about autism, and foster a culture of inclusivity and empathy. Through increased awareness and understanding, supportive communities work towards eliminating stigma and creating environments where individuals with autism are valued for their unique strengths and contributions.

5. Encouraging Peer Support: Supportive communities and networks encourage peer support among individuals with autism. Peer support involves connecting individuals with shared experiences, providing opportunities for mutual learning, and fostering a sense of solidarity. Peer support can enhance self-confidence, social skills, and self-advocacy in individuals with autism.

6. Advocacy and Collaboration: Supportive communities and networks engage in advocacy efforts and collaborate with stakeholders to promote the rights and well-being of individuals with autism. They work towards influencing policies, improving access to services, and creating inclusive environments. Advocacy and collaboration ensure that the voices of individuals with autism are heard and that their needs and concerns are addressed.

7. Celebrating Diversity: Supportive communities and networks celebrate the diversity of individuals with autism and promote an inclusive mindset. They recognize that each individual has unique strengths, abilities, and perspectives. By celebrating diversity, supportive communities foster an environment where individuals with autism can thrive, contribute, and be celebrated for who they are.

Supportive communities and networks play a crucial role in enhancing the social, emotional, and overall well-being of individuals with autism. They provide a sense of belonging, support, and understanding, and promote an inclusive society that values the contributions of individuals with autism. By building supportive communities and networks, society can create an environment where individuals with autism can lead fulfilling lives and reach their full potential.

5. Legislation and Policy:

The main point of the chapter section on "Legislation and Policy" is to highlight the importance of enacting comprehensive legislation and implementing effective policies that protect the rights and promote the well-being of individuals with autism. It emphasizes the role of legislation and policy in creating a supportive legal framework that ensures access to necessary services, supports inclusive education and employment, and addresses the unique needs and challenges faced by individuals with autism. The main points related to legislation and policy can be explained as follows:

1. Legal Protection and Rights: The chapter emphasizes the significance of legislation in providing legal protection and upholding the rights of individuals with autism. It

highlights the importance of laws that prevent discrimination, ensure equal access to opportunities, and protect individuals with autism from harm or neglect. Legal protection and rights-based legislation help create a foundation for inclusivity and empower individuals with autism to assert their rights.

2. Access to Services and Supports: The chapter addresses the need for legislation and policy that ensures individuals with autism have access to necessary services and supports. This includes healthcare, therapeutic interventions, educational accommodations, vocational training, and other resources that promote their overall well-being and development. Legislation can establish guidelines and mechanisms to ensure the availability, affordability, and quality of these services.

3. Inclusive Education: The chapter emphasizes the importance of legislation and policy that promotes inclusive education for individuals with autism. It highlights the need for laws that guarantee equal access to education, encourage inclusive practices in schools, and

provide necessary supports and accommodations to facilitate the learning and development of individuals with autism. Inclusive education legislation helps create inclusive learning environments where individuals with autism can thrive academically and socially.

4. Employment Opportunities: The chapter addresses the role of legislation and policy in promoting employment opportunities for individuals with autism. It emphasizes the need for laws that prevent discrimination in the workplace, promote reasonable accommodations, and encourage inclusive hiring practices. Employment-related legislation helps create a supportive and inclusive labor market where individuals with autism can participate fully and contribute their unique skills and talents.

5. Research Funding and Initiatives: The chapter recognizes the importance of legislation and policy that supports research funding and initiatives in the field of autism. It emphasizes the need for laws that allocate resources for autism research, encourage collaboration among researchers and institutions, and promote the

dissemination of research findings. Research-focused legislation helps advance knowledge about autism, inform evidence-based practices, and improve the understanding of the needs and potential of individuals with autism.

6. Collaboration and Coordination:

"Collaboration and Coordination" is to highlight the importance of fostering collaboration and coordination among various stakeholders involved in supporting individuals with autism. It emphasizes the need for cooperation, shared responsibility, and effective communication among government agencies, healthcare professionals, educators, families, and advocacy organizations. The main points related to collaboration and coordination can be explained as follows:

1. Multi-Sectoral Collaboration: The chapter emphasizes the significance of collaboration among stakeholders from different sectors involved in supporting individuals with autism. This includes government agencies, healthcare providers, educators, community organizations, and families. Collaborative efforts enable the pooling of

resources, expertise, and perspectives to address the diverse needs of individuals with autism comprehensively.

2. Information Sharing: Collaboration and coordination facilitate the sharing of information among stakeholders. This includes sharing research findings, best practices, resources, and experiences related to autism. By sharing information, stakeholders can learn from one another, stay updated on advancements in the field, and ensure a consistent and evidence-based approach to supporting individuals with autism.

3. Coordinated Support Systems: Effective collaboration and coordination help establish coordinated support systems for individuals with autism. This involves aligning services, interventions, and supports across various domains, such as healthcare, education, employment, and community services. Coordinated support systems ensure that individuals with autism receive comprehensive and seamless support tailored to their unique needs.

4. Comprehensive Assessment and Planning: Collaboration and coordination allow for comprehensive assessment and planning for individuals with autism. By bringing together different perspectives and expertise, stakeholders can conduct thorough assessments, identify strengths and challenges, and develop individualized plans that address the diverse needs of individuals with autism across various domains of their lives.

5. Early Intervention and Transition: Collaboration and coordination are particularly crucial during early intervention and transition periods in the lives of individuals with autism. Stakeholders must work together to ensure timely and appropriate early intervention services for young children with autism and facilitate smooth transitions from early intervention to school and from school to post-secondary education or employment. Collaborative efforts support continuity of care and minimize disruptions during these critical life stages.

6. Shared Responsibility: Collaboration and coordination promote shared responsibility among stakeholders in

supporting individuals with autism. Each stakeholder has a role to play, and by working together, they can effectively address the complex and diverse needs of individuals with autism. Shared responsibility ensures that support is holistic, comprehensive, and responsive to the evolving needs of individuals with autism.

7. Advocacy and Policy Development: Collaboration and coordination are essential in advocacy efforts and policy development. By coming together, stakeholders can advocate for the rights and needs of individuals with autism, influence policies and legislation, and promote systemic changes that improve the lives of individuals with autism and their families. Collaboration in advocacy and policy development ensures a unified voice and a stronger impact.

Effective collaboration and coordination among stakeholders are essential for creating a supportive and inclusive environment for individuals with autism. By fostering collaboration, sharing information, and coordinating support systems, stakeholders can ensure a comprehensive and holistic approach to supporting individuals with autism across various domains of their lives. Collaboration and coordination enable stakeholders to leverage their expertise and resources to maximize positive outcomes and improve the overall well-being of individuals with autism.

7. Continuous Evaluation and Improvement: The chapter addresses the need for legislation and policy that promotes continuous evaluation and improvement of support systems and services for individuals with autism. It emphasizes the importance of laws that mandate regular assessment, review, and updates of existing policies to align with emerging research, best practices, and the evolving needs of the autism community. Evaluation-focused legislation ensures that support systems remain responsive, effective, and adaptable to changing circumstances.

Legislation and policy play a crucial role in shaping the legal and social landscape for individuals with autism. By enacting comprehensive legislation and implementing effective policies, society can create a supportive and inclusive environment that upholds the rights, promotes access to services, ensures inclusive education and employment, and addresses the unique needs and challenges of individuals with autism.

6. Research and Innovation: The chapter recognizes the significance of ongoing research and innovation in advancing the understanding of autism and developing effective interventions and support strategies. It discusses the need for continued investment in research, exploring new technologies, and promoting evidence-based practices that enhance the quality of life for individuals with autism.

7. Advocacy and Collaboration: The chapter emphasizes the power of advocacy and collaboration in shaping a future of empowerment for individuals with autism. It encourages individuals, families, professionals, organizations, and communities to work together to challenge barriers, influence policies, raise awareness, and create opportunities that promote the rights, well-being, and inclusion of individuals with autism.

Conclusion

As I reflect upon my personal experience and the knowledge I have gained on the subject of collaboration and coordination in supporting individuals with autism, I am filled with a deep sense of appreciation for the power of working together. Throughout this journey, I have witnessed firsthand the transformative impact that collaboration and coordination can have on the lives of individuals with autism and their families.

I recall the moments when I first realized the importance of bringing stakeholders from different sectors together. It was through collaboration that I saw healthcare professionals, educators, government agencies, and advocacy organizations pooling their expertise and resources to create a more comprehensive and holistic support system. By sharing information and learning from one another's experiences, we were able to develop a deeper understanding of the diverse needs of individuals with autism and develop strategies that addressed these needs effectively.

In my personal experience, collaboration and coordination have played a vital role in ensuring that no aspect of support for individuals with autism is overlooked. Through coordinated efforts, we have been able to create a network of support that spans across healthcare, education, employment, and community services. The power of collaboration has enabled us to align services, interventions, and supports, providing individuals with autism with a seamless and integrated support system that promotes their well-being and development.

I have also witnessed the tremendous impact of collaboration during critical transition periods in the lives of individuals with autism. The coordinated efforts of stakeholders have facilitated smooth transitions from early intervention programs to schools and from schools to post-secondary education or employment. This continuity of care has been instrumental in minimizing disruptions and ensuring that individuals with autism receive the support they need to thrive in various stages of their lives.

Through collaboration, I have seen the power of shared responsibility. Each stakeholder has brought their unique strengths, perspectives, and expertise to the table, contributing to a collective effort to support individuals with autism. This shared responsibility has fostered a sense of unity and purpose, reminding us that we are all working towards a common goal: the empowerment and well-being of individuals with autism.

Finally, collaboration and coordination have fueled our advocacy efforts and policy development. By coming together as a unified force, we have been able to advocate for the rights and needs of individuals with autism, influencing policies and bringing about systemic changes. Through collaboration, we have amplified our voices and achieved meaningful advancements that have improved the lives of individuals with autism and their families.

As I conclude this personal reflection on collaboration and coordination, I am filled with hope and inspiration. The journey of supporting individuals with autism is not a solitary one but a collective effort that requires the collaboration and coordination of diverse stakeholders. It is through these collaborative efforts that we can create a society that embraces neurodiversity, provides inclusive support systems, and empowers individuals with autism to live fulfilling lives.

I am grateful for the opportunities I have had to collaborate with passionate individuals and organizations dedicated to making a difference in the lives of individuals with autism. Together, we have learned, grown, and achieved more than we ever could have individually. As I continue on this journey, I carry with me the profound understanding that collaboration and coordination are the keys to unlocking the full potential of individuals with autism and building a more inclusive and accepting society for all.

Manufactured by Amazon.ca
Acheson, AB